the **Boxer**

A guide to selection, care, nutrition,
upbringing, training, health, breeding,
sports and play.

Contents

Foreword

The book you are holding is a basic 'owner's manual'
for everyone owning a Boxer and also for those who
are considering buying a Boxer. What we have done in
this book is to give the basic information to help the
(future) owner of a Boxer look after his or her pet
responsibly. Too many people still buy a pet before
really understanding what they're about to get into.

If you are interested in more information available
about this breed, its in-depth history and development,
feeding, training, health, ailments and whatever else,
other more extensive books are available in book stores
and pet shops.

This book goes into the broad history of the Boxer,
the breed standard and some pros and cons of buying
a Boxer. You will also find essential information on
feeding, initial training and an introduction to
reproduction. Finally we give attention to (day-by-day)
care, health and some breed-specific ailments.

Based on this information, you can buy a Boxer,
having thought it through carefully, and keep it as a pet
in a responsible manner. Our advice, though, is not just
to leave it to this small book. A properly brought-up
and well-trained dog is more than just a dog. Invest a
little extra in a puppy training course or an obedience
course. There are also excellent books available that go
deeper into certain aspects than is possible here.

About Pets

about pets

A Publication of About Pets.

Copyright © 2003
About Pets
co-publisher United Kingdom
Kingdom Books
PO9 5TL, England

ISBN 1852791829
First printing September 2003
Second printing May 2004
Third printing April 2005

Original title: *de Boxer*
© 2002 Welzo Media Productions bv,
About Pets bv
Warffum, the Netherlands
http://www.overdieren.nl

Photos:
Rob Doolaard, Rob Dekker,
Bayer, Virbac, Europet, Fons Geerlings,
Loes van Nieuwland, Iris Boots,
Henry Beuks, Mr. Kolk, M. Jasper
and other members of the
Boxer Club of the Netherlands.

Printed in China through Printworks Int. Ltd.

In general

This breed that originated in Germany is now spread across the world and has countless fans. In this country too, the Boxer has been a popular breed of dog for many years.

Origins

The history of the Boxer does not really go very far back. The Boxer, just as the Bulldog and Mastiff, is a descendant of fighting dogs from the Middle Ages. One of these, the "Brabant Bull Biter", is regarded as the ancestor of today's Boxer. The advantage behind its appearance is that with its drawn-back nose it could keep breathing while hanging on to the bull.

Targeted breeding of these dogs only began at the end of the 19th century. When breeding its sunken nose, man was helped by a play of nature called chondrodystrophy. This arises from unique deformities because the cartilage does not solidify. The base of the skull remains short, but the roof of the skull develops well, the nose does

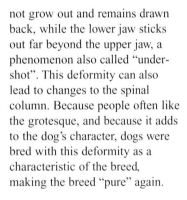

not grow out and remains drawn back, while the lower jaw sticks out far beyond the upper jaw, a phenomenon also called "under-shot". This deformity can also lead to changes to the spinal column. Because people often like the grotesque, and because it adds to the dog's character, dogs were bred with this deformity as a characteristic of the breed, making the breed "pure" again.

The first Boxer association was founded in Germany in 1896, and similar associations then were founded around Europe. Even before the First World War, breeders were able to achieve a good deal of uniformity in the breed. This was thanks, above all, to Mrs. Friederun Stockmann with her "Von Dom" kennels.

At international level also, one understood the importance of co-operation. In Europe Atibox (Association Technique Internationale du Boxer) was founded in 1968. This international organisation's annual show, held each year in a different member country, is regarded as the high point on the Boxer calendar. Atibox also organises international training competitions at the highest level.

Much use is still made in many countries of the Boxer's original characteristics as a guard and defence dog. The Boxer is trained as a guide dog for the blind in some countries and various types of competition have become more popular over the past few years. Even if the Boxer is not the easiest or most successful breed in this field, both the dog and its master get a lot of pleasure from this type of sport.

Breed standard

A standard has been developed for all breeds recognised by the Kennel Club for the UK (and in Europe by the F.C.I. - the umbrella organisation for western European kennel clubs). Officially approved kennel clubs in the member countries provide a translation. This standard provides a guideline for breeders and judges. It is something of an ideal that dogs of the breed must strive to match. With some breeds, dogs are already bred that match the ideal. Other breeds have a long way to go. There is a list of defects for each breed. These can be serious defects that disqualify the dog, and it will be excluded from breeding. Permitted defects are not serious, but do cost points in a show.

The UK Kennel Club breed standard for the Boxer

General Appearance

Great nobility, smooth-coated, medium-sized, square build, strong bone and evident, well developed muscles.

Characteristics

Lively, strong, loyal to owner and family, but distrustful of strangers. Obedient, friendly at play, but with guarding instinct.

Temperament

Equable, biddable, fearless, self-assured.

Head and Skull

Head imparts its unique individual stamp and is in proportion to body, appearing neither light nor too heavy. Skull lean without exaggerated cheek muscles. Muzzle broad, deep and powerful, never narrow, pointed, short or shallow. Balance of skull and muzzle essential, with muzzle never appearing small, viewed from any angle. Skull cleanly covered, showing no wrinkle, except when alerted. Creases present

Docked tail

Undocked tail

from root of nose running down sides of muzzle. Dark mask confined to muzzle, distinctly contrasting with colour of head, even when white is present. Lower jaw undershot, curving slightly upward. Upper jaw broad where attached to skull, tapering very slightly to front. Muzzle shape completed by upper lips, thick and well padded, supported by well separated canine teeth of lower jaw. Lower edge of upper lip rests on edge of lower lip, so that chin is clearly perceptible when viewed from front or side. Lower jaw never to obscure front of upper lip, neither should teeth nor tongue be visible when mouth closed. Top of skull slightly arched, not rounded, nor too flat and broad. Occiput not too pronounced. Distinct stop, bridge of nose

never forced back into forehead, nor should it be downfaced. Length of muzzle measured from tip of nose to inside corner of eye is one-third length of head measured from tip of nose to occiput. Nose broad, black, slightly turned up, wide nostrils with well defined line between. Tip of nose set slightly higher than root of muzzle. Cheeks powerfully developed, never bulging.

Eyes
Dark brown, forward looking, not too small, protruding or deeply set. Showing lively, intelligent expression. Dark rims with good pigmentation showing no haw.

Ears
Moderate size, thin, set wide apart on highest part of skull lying flat and close to cheek in repose, but

falling forward with definite crease when alert.

Mouth

Undershot jaw, canines set wide apart with incisors (six) in straight line in lower jaw. In upper jaw set in line curving slightly forward. Bite powerful and sound, with teeth set in normal arrangement.

Neck

Round, of ample length, strong, muscular, clean cut, no dewlap. Distinctly marked nape and elegant arch down to withers.

Forequarters

Shoulders long and sloping, close lying, not excessively covered with muscle. Upper arm long, making right angle to shoulderblade. Forelegs seen from front, straight, parallel, with strong bone. Elbows not too close or standing too far from chest wall. Forearms perpendicular, long and firmly muscled. Pasterns short, clearly defined, but not distended, slightly slanted.

Body

In profile square, length from forechest to rear of upper thigh

equal to height at withers. Chest deep, reaching to elbows. Depth of chest half height at withers. Ribs well arched, not barrel-shaped, extending well to rear. Withers clearly defined. Back short, straight, slightly sloping, broad and strongly muscled. Loin short, well tucked up and taut. Lower abdominal line blends into curve to rear.

Hindquarters
Very strong with muscles hard and standing out noticeably under skin. Thighs broad and curved. Broad croup slightly sloped, with flat, broad arch. Pelvis long and broad. Upper and lower thigh long. Good hind angulation; when standing, the stifle is directly under the hip protuberance. Seen from side, leg from hock joint to foot not quite vertical. Seen from

behind, legs straight, hock joints clean, with powerful rear pads.

Feet
Front feet small and cat-like, with well arched toes, and hard pads; hind feet slightly longer.

Tail
Customarily docked.
Docked: Set on high and carried upward.
Undocked: Set on high and carried gaily, not curled over back. Of moderate thickness. In overall balance to the rest of dog.

Gait/Movement
Strong, powerful with noble bearing, reaching well forward, and with driving action of hindquarters. In profile, stride free and ground covering.

Coat
Short, glossy, smooth and tight to body.

Colour
Fawn or brindle. White markings acceptable not exceeding one-third of ground colour.
Fawn: Various shades from dark deer red to light fawn.
Brindle: Black stripes on previously described fawn shades, running parallel to ribs all over body. Stripes contrast distinctly to ground colour, neither too close nor too thinly dispersed. Ground colour clear, not intermingling with stripes.

Size
Height: dogs: 57-63 cms (22.5-25 ins); bitches: 53-59 cms (21-23 ins).

Weight: dogs: approximately 30-32 kgs (66-70 lbs); bitches: approximately 25-27 kgs (55-60 lbs).

Faults
Any departure from the foregoing points should be considered a fault and the seriousness with which the fault should be regarded should be in exact proportion to its degree and its effect upon the health and welfare of the dog.

Note
Male animals should have two apparently normal testicles fully descended into the scrotum.

Breed standard by courtesy of the Kennel Club of Great Britain

Buying a Boxer

Once you've made that properly considered decision to buy a dog, there are several options. Should it be a puppy, an adult dog, or even an older dog? Should it be a bitch or dog, a pedigree dog or a cross?

Of course, the question also comes up as to where to buy your dog - from a private person, a reliable breeder or an animal shelter? For you and the animal, it's vital to get these questions sorted out in advance. You want a dog that will suit your circumstances properly. With a puppy, you get a playful energetic housemate that will easily adapt to a new environment. If you want something quieter, an older dog is a good choice.

Pros and cons of the Boxer

The Boxer is a medium-sized, smooth-coated dog with a noble and liberal character. Although it was originally a guard and fighting dog, the Boxer is affectionate and loyal to its companions, and its love of children is well-known. These characteristics make the Boxer a pleasant housedog.

The Boxer is a late developer that needs time to develop. Remember that Boxers, despite their in-born pleasant nature, are more than a little physically strong. Furthermore, Boxers can be enormously stubborn. A rigorous upbringing is thus required.

With its friendly, happy and often clown-like character, the Boxer knows how to make friends. Because of its protruding upper lip, the Boxer has more of a tendency to dribble at the mouth than other dogs with tightly fitting lips. A Boxer is not a suitable breed to run up and down stairs because of the risk of hip dysplasia and vulnerability to rheumatism.

If you live in an upstairs flat with no lift, you would do better to choose another breed.

No-one can deny a certain inquisitiveness in this dog. A Boxer will remain playful and active right up to the end of its life, it's always in for a game with a ball or stick and will enjoy a long walk. Because of their temperament, Boxers like to be 'busy'. Despite being active and insatiable for exercise, the Boxer does have a tendency to get fat, but with enough exercise it will be quiet in the home and it is certainly not an excessive barker. It will enjoy being involved in family events, and if it's not getting enough attention it will certainly make that known.

Many take advantage of their Boxer's enthusiasm by practising agility or flyball. Boxers are also suitable for obedience training, even if they do keep a good portion of their obstinate and stubborn nature. A Boxer will not be a star in competitions.

Male or female?

Whether you choose a male or a female puppy, or an adult dog or bitch, is an entirely personal decision. A male typically needs more leadership because he tends to be more dominant by nature. He will try to play boss over other dogs and, if he gets the chance, over people too. In the wild, the most dominant dog (or wolf) is

always the leader of the pack. In many cases this is a male. A bitch is much more focussed on her master, she sees him as the pack leader.

A puppy test is good for defining the kind of character a young dog will develop. During a test one usually sees that a dog is more dominant than a bitch. You can often quickly recognise the bossy, the adventurous and the cautious characters. So visit the litter a couple of times early on. Try to pick a puppy that suits your own personality. A dominant dog, for instance, needs a strong hand. It will often try to see how far it can go. You must regularly make it clear who's the boss, and that it must obey all the members of the family. The breeder can give you good advice on this point. He or she knows the puppies and will recommend a pup that suits you and your family.

When bitches are sexually mature, they will go into season. On average, a bitch is in season twice a year for about two or three weeks. This is the fertile period when she can become pregnant. Particularly in the second half of her season, she will want to go looking for a dog to mate with. A male dog will show more masculine traits once he is sexually mature. He will make sure other dogs know what territory is his by urinating as

often as possible in as many places as he can. He is also difficult to restrain if there's a bitch in season nearby. As far as normal care is concerned there is little difference between a dog and a bitch.

Puppy or adult?

After you've made the decision for a male or female, the next question comes up. Should it be a puppy or an adult dog? Your household circumstances usually play a major role here.

Of course, it's great having a sweet little puppy in the house, but bringing up a young dog requires a lot of time. In the first year of its life it learns more than during the rest of its life. This is the period when the foundations are laid for elementary matters such as house-training, obedience and social behaviour. You must reckon with the fact that your puppy will keep you busy for a couple of hours a day, certainly in the first few months. You won't need so much time with a grown

dog. It has already been brought up, but this doesn't mean it won't need correcting from time to time.

A puppy will no doubt leave a trail of destruction in its wake for the first few months. With a little bad luck, this will cost you a number of rolls of wallpaper, some good shoes and a few socks. In the worst case you'll be left with some chewed furniture. Some puppies even manage to tear curtains from their rails. With good upbringing this 'vandalism' will quickly disappear, but you won't have to worry about this if you get an older dog.

The greatest advantage of a puppy, of course, is that you can bring it up your own way. And the upbringing a dog gets (or doesn't get) is a major influence on its whole character. Finally, financial aspects may play a role in your choice. A puppy is generally (much) more expensive than an adult dog, not only in purchase price but also in 'maintenance'. A puppy needs to go to the vet's more often for the necessary vaccinations and check-ups.

Overall, bringing up a puppy requires a good deal of energy, time and money, but you have its upbringing in your own hands. An adult dog involves less money and time, but its character is already formed. You should also try to find out about the background of

an adult dog. Its previous owner may have formed its character in somewhat less positive ways.

Two dogs?

Having two or more dogs in the house is not just nice for us, but also for the animals themselves. Dogs get a lot of pleasure from their own company. After all, they are pack animals.

If you're sure that you want two young dogs, it's best not to buy them at the same time. Bringing a dog up and establishing the bond between dog and master takes time, and you need to give a lot of attention to your dog in this phase. Having two puppies in the house means you have to divide your attention between them. Apart from that, there's a danger that they will focus on one another rather than on their master. Buy the second pup when the first is (almost) an adult.

Getting a puppy when the first dog is somewhat older often has a positive effect on the older dog. The influence of the puppy almost seems to give it a second childhood. The older dog, if it's been well brought up, can help with the upbringing of the puppy. Young dogs like to imitate the behaviour of their elders. Don't forget to give both dogs the same amount of attention. Take both out alone at least once per day during the first eighteen months. Give the older dog enough opportunity to get some peace and quiet. It won't want an enthusiastic youngster running around under its feet all the time. Moreover, a puppy needs plenty of sleep and may have to have the brakes put on it once in a while.

Two adult dogs can happily be brought into the home together, as long as they're used to each other. If this is not the case, then they have to go through that process. This is usually best achieved by letting them get to know each other on neutral territory. This prevents fights for territory. On neutral territory, perhaps an acquaintance's garden where neither dog has been before, both dogs are basically equal. Once they've got to know each other, you can take them both home, and they can sort out the hierarchy there amongst themselves. In any event, don't get involved in trying to 'arbitrate'. That is human, but for the dog that's at the top of the pecking order it's like having its position undone. It will only make the dog more dominant in behaviour, with all the consequences. Once the hierarchy is established, most dogs can get along fine together.

The combination of a male and female needs special attention and it's good advice to get a second dog of the same sex. This will avoid a lot of problems. Sterilisation and castration is, of

course, one solution, but it's a final one. A sterilised or castrated animal can never reproduce.

A dog and children

Dogs and children are a great combination. They can play together and get great pleasure out of each other's company. Moreover, children need to learn how to handle living beings; they develop respect and a sense of responsibility by caring for a dog (or other pets). However sweet a dog is, children must understand that it is an animal and not a toy. A dog isn't comfortable when it's being messed around with. It can become frightened, timid and even aggressive. So make it clear what a dog likes and what it doesn't. Look for ways the child can play with the dog, perhaps a game of hide-and-seek where the child hides and the dog has to find it. Even a simple tennis ball can give enormous pleasure. Children must learn to leave a dog in peace when it doesn't want to play any more. The dog must also have its own place where it's not disturbed. Have children help with your dog's care as much as possible. A strong bond will be the result. The arrival of a baby also means changes in the life of a dog. Before the birth you can help get the dog acquainted with the new situation. Let it sniff at the new things in the house and it will quickly accept them. When the baby has arrived involve the dog as much as possible in day-by-day events, but make sure it gets plenty of attention too. NEVER leave a dog alone with young children. Crawling infants sometimes make unexpected movements, which can easily frighten a dog. And infants are hugely curious, and may try to find out whether the tail is really fastened to the dog, or whether its eyes come out, just like they do with their cuddly toys. But a dog is a dog and it will defend itself when it feels threatened.

Where to buy

There are various ways of acquiring a dog. The decision for a puppy or an adult dog will also define for the most part where to buy your dog.

If it's to be a puppy, then you need to find a breeder with a litter. If you chose a popular breed, like the Boxer, there is choice enough. But you may also face the problem that there are so many puppies on sale that have only been bred for profit's sake. You can see how many puppies are for sale by looking in the regional newspaper every Saturday. Some of these dogs have a pedigree, but many don't. These breeders very often don't watch out for breed-specific illnesses and any hereditary breeding faults and defects; puppies are separated from their mother as fast as possible and are thus insufficiently socialised. Never buy a puppy that is too young, or whose mother you weren't able to see.

Fortunately there are also enough bonafide breeders of Boxers who have been involved with the breed for many years as serious breeders and exhibitors and these are only too willing to help you get your Boxer.

Try to visit a number of breeders before you actually buy your puppy. Check the parent dogs' papers to ensure they were free of Hip Dysplasia (HD) and of heart defects. Ask if the breeder is prepared to help you after you've bought your puppy, and to help you find solutions for any problems that may come up.

The breed clubs may be able to inform you about available puppies of breeders who are members of the association. They will often publish lists of litters that have been bred according to their guidelines. To be recognised as a breeder by the breed associations, a breeder must fulfil certain requirements, such as the parents should be heart tested and have grades no more than grade 1.

Finally, you should understand that a pedigree is nothing more or less than evidence of descent. Breeder clubs will also issue pedigrees for offspring of dogs that suffer from hereditary disorders, or that have not been examined for them. A pedigree tells you nothing about the health of the parent dogs.

If you're looking for an adult dog, it's best to contact the breed association, who often help place adult dogs that can no longer be kept by their owners because of personal circumstances (impulse buying, moving home, divorce etc.).

Things to watch out for

Buying a puppy is no simple matter. You must pay attention to the following:

* Never buy a puppy on impulse, even if it is love at first sight. A dog is a living being that will need care and attention over a long period. It is not a toy that you can put away when you're finished with it.
* Take a good look at the mother. Is she calm, nervous, aggressive, well cared-for or neglected? The behaviour and condition of the mother is not only a sign of the quality of the breeder, but also of the puppy you're about to buy.
* Avoid buying a puppy whose mother has been kept only in a kennel. A young dog needs as many different impressions as possible in its first few months, including living in a family group. It gets used to people and possibly other pets. Kennel dogs miss these experiences and are inadequately socialised.
* Always ask to see the parents' papers (vaccination certificates, pedigrees, and official reports on health examinations).
* Never buy a puppy younger than eight weeks.
* Put all agreements with the breeder in writing. A model agreement is available from the Kennel Club.

Travelling with your Boxer

There are a few things to think about before travelling with your dog. While one Boxer may enjoy travelling, another may hate it. You may like holidays in far-away places, but it's questionable whether your dog will enjoy them as much.

That very first trip

The first trip of a Boxer puppy's life is also the most nerve-wrecking. This is the trip from the breeder's to its new home. If you can, pick up your puppy in the early morning. Then it will have plenty of time to get used to its new surroundings. Ask the breeder not to feed the puppy that day. The young animal will be overwhelmed by all kinds of new experiences. Firstly, it's away from its mother; it's in a small room (the car) with all its different smells, noises and strange people. So there's a big chance that the puppy will be car-sick this first time, with the annoying consequence that it will remember travelling in the car as an unpleasant experience. So it's important to make this first trip as pleasant as possible.

When picking up a puppy, always take someone with you who can sit in the back seat with the puppy on his or her lap and talk to it calmly. If it's too warm for the puppy, a place on the floor at the feet of your companion is ideal. The pup will lie there relatively quietly and may even take a nap. Ask the breeder for a cloth or something else from the puppies' basket or bed that carries a familiar scent. The puppy can lie on this in the car, and it will also help if it feels lonely during the first nights at home.

If the trip home is a long one, then stop for a break (once in a while). Let your puppy roam and sniff around (on the lead!), offer it a little drink and, if necessary, let it do its business. Do take care to lay an old towel in the car. It can

happen that the puppy, in its nervousness, may urinate or be sick. It's also good advice to give a puppy positive experiences with car journeys. Make short trips to nice places where you can walk and play with it. It can be a real nuisance if your dog doesn't like travelling in a car. After all, once in a while you will have to take it to certain places, such as the vet's or to visit friends and acquaintances.

Taking your Boxer on holiday

When making holiday plans, you also need to think about what you're going to do with your dog during that time. Are you taking it with you, putting it into kennels or leaving it with friends? In any event there are a number of things you need to do in good time.

If you want to take your Boxer with you, you need to be sure in advance that it will be welcome at your holiday home, and what rules there are. If you're going abroad it will need certain vaccinations and a health certificate, which normally need to be done four weeks before departure. You must also be sure that you've made all the arrangements necessary to bring your dog back home to the UK, without it needing to go into quarantine under the rabies regulations. Your vet can give you the most recent information.

If your trip is to southern Europe, ask for a treatment against ticks (you can read more about this in the chapter on Parasites). Although dog-owners usually enjoy taking their dog on holiday, you must seriously ask yourself whether the dog feels that way too. Boxers certainly don't always feel comfortable in a hot country. Days spent travelling in a car are also often not their preference, and some dogs suffer badly from car-sickness. There are good medicines for this, but it's questionable whether you're doing your dog a favour with them. If you do decide to take it with you, make regular stops at safe places during your journey, so that your dog can have a good run. Take plenty of fresh drinking water with you, as well as the food your dog is used to. Don't leave your dog in a car that is parked in the sun. It can quickly be overcome by the heat, with even fatal consequences. If you can't avoid it, park the car in the shade if at all possible, and leave a window open for a little fresh air. Even if you've taken these precautions, never stay away long!

If you're travelling by plane or ship, make sure in good time that your dog can travel with you and what rules you need to observe. You will need some time to make all the arrangements. Maybe you decide not to take your dog with you, and you then need to find somewhere for it to stay. Arrangements for a place in kennels need to be made well in advance, and there may be certain vaccinations required, which need to be given a minimum of one month before the stay.

If your dog can't be accommodated in the homes of relatives or friends, it might be possible to have an acquaintance stay in your house. This also needs to be arranged well in advance, as it may be difficult to find someone that can do this.

Always ensure that your dog can be traced should it run away or get lost while on holiday. A little tube with your address or a tag with home and holiday address can prevent a lot of problems.

Moving home

Dogs generally become more attached to humans than to the house they live in. Moving home is usually not a problem for them. But it can be useful before moving to let the dog get to know its new home and the area around it.

If you can, leave your dog with relatives or friends (or in kennels) on the day of the move. The chance of it running away or getting lost is then practically non-existent. When your move is complete, you can pick your dog up and let it quietly get familiar with its new home and environment. Give it its own place in the house at once and it will quickly adapt. During the first week or so, always walk your dog on a lead because an animal can also get lost in new surroundings. Always take a different route so it quickly gets to know the neighbourhood.

Don't forget to get your new address and phone number engraved on the dog's tag. Send a change of address notice to the institution that has any chip or tattoo data. Dogs must sometimes be registered in a new community.

Nutrition, feeding your Boxer

A dog will actually eat a lot more than just meat. In the wild it would eat its prey complete with skin and fur, including the bones, stomach, and the innards with their semi-digested vegetable material.

In this way the dog supplements its meat menu with the vitamins and minerals it needs. This is also the basis for feeding a domestic dog.

Ready-made foods

It's not easy for a layman to put together a complete menu for a dog, that includes all the necessary proteins, fats, vitamins and minerals in just the right proportions and quantities. Meat alone is certainly not a complete meal for a dog. It contains too little calcium. A calcium deficiency over time will lead to bone defects, and for a fast-growing puppy this can lead to serious skeletal deformities.

If you mix its food yourself, you can easily give your dog too much in terms of vitamins and minerals, which can also be bad for your

dog's health. You can avoid these problems by giving it ready-made food of a good brand. These products are well balanced and contain everything your dog needs. Supplements such as vitamin preparations are superfluous. The amount of food your dog needs depends on its weight and activity level. You can find guidelines on the packaging. Split the food into two meals per day if possible, and always ensure there's a bowl of fresh drinking water next to its food.

Give your dog the time to digest its food, don't let it outside straight after a meal. A dog should also never play on a full stomach. This can cause stomach torsion (the stomach turning over), which can be fatal for your dog.

Because the nutritional needs of a dog depend, among other things, on its age and way of life, there are many different types of dog food available. There are "light" foods for less active dogs, "energy" foods for working dogs and "senior" foods for the older dog.

Puppy chunks

There is now a wide assortment of puppy chunks on the market. These chunks contain a higher content of growth-promoting nutrients, such as protein and calcium. For medium-sized breeds such as the Boxer however, these chunks can actually be harmful. The dog will grow fast enough, and faster growth will only promote conditions such as Hip and Elbow Dysplasia (see the chapter Your Boxer's health). Give your puppy only special puppy chunks for larger breeds.

Canned foods, mixer and dry foods

Ready-made foods available at pet shops or in the supermarket can roughly be split into canned food, mixer and dry food. Whichever form you choose, ensure that it's a complete food with all the necessary ingredients. You can see this on the packaging.

Most dogs love canned food. Although the better brands are composed well, they do have one disadvantage: they are soft.

A dog fed only on canned food will sooner or later have problems with its teeth (plaque, paradontosis). Besides canned food, give your dog hard foods at certain times or a dog chew, such as Nylabone Healthy Edibles.

Mixer is a food consisting of chunks, dried vegetables and grains. Almost all moisture has been extracted. The advantages of mixer are that it is light and keeps well. You add a certain amount of water and the meal is ready. A disadvantage is that it must definitely not be fed without water. Without the extra fluid, mixer will absorb the fluids present in the stomach, with serious results. Should your dog manage to get at the bag and enjoy its contents, you must immediately give it plenty to drink.

Dry chunks have also had the moisture extracted but not as much as mixer. The advantage of dry foods is that they are hard, forcing the dog to use its jaws, removing plaque and massaging the gums.

Dog chew products

Of course, once in a while you want to spoil your dog with something extra. Don't give it pieces of cheese or sausage as these contain too much salt and fat. There are various products available that a dog will find delicious and which are also healthy, especially for its teeth. You'll find a large range of varying quality in the pet shop. Remember that your Boxer will have a tendency to dribble because of its protruding upper lip. Do not give extras at fixed times, or when you are eating as this excites saliva production. This also avoids the dog begging.

The butcher's left-overs

The bones of slaughtered animals have traditionally been given to the dog and dogs love them, but they are not without risks. Pork and poultry bones are too weak. They can splinter and cause serious injury to the intestines. Beef bones are more suitable, but they must first be cooked to kill off dangerous bacteria. Pet shops carry a range of smoked, cooked and dried abattoir residue, such as pigs' ears, bull penis, tripe sticks, oxtails, gullet, dried muscle meat, and hoof chews.

Buffalo or cowhide chews

Dog chews are mostly made of cowhide or buffalo hide. Chews are usually knotted or pressed hide and can come in the form of little shoes, twisted sticks, lollies, balls and various other shapes; nice to look at and a nice change.

Munchy sticks

Munchy sticks are green, yellow, red or brown coloured sticks of various thicknesses. They consist of ground buffalo hide with a

Fresh meat

If you do want to give your dog fresh meat occasionally, never give it raw, but always boiled or roasted. Raw (or not fully cooked) pork or chicken can contain life-threatening bacteria. Chicken can be contaminated by the notorious salmonella bacteria, while pork can carry the Aujeszky virus. This disease is incurable and will quickly lead to the death of your pet.

number of often undefined additives. The composition and quality of these between-meal treats is not always clear. Some are fine, but there have also been sticks found to contain high levels of cardboard and even paint residues. Choose a product whose ingredients are clearly described.

Something to drink

A dog can go days without eating if it must, but definitely not without drinking! Make sure it always has a bowl of fresh water available. Food and water bowls of stainless steel are the easiest to keep clean.

Overweight?

Recent investigations have shown that many dogs are overweight. A dog usually gets too fat because of over-feeding and lack of exercise. Use of medicines or a disease is rarely the cause. Dogs that get too fat are often given too much food or treats between meals. Gluttony

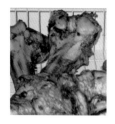

or boredom can also be a cause, and a dog often puts on weight following castration or sterilisation. Due to changes in hormone levels, it becomes less active and consumes less energy. Finally, simply too little exercise alone can lead to a dog becoming overweight.

You can use the following rule of thumb to check whether your Boxer is overweight: you should be able to see its ribs if the dog is standing in a somewhat twisted posture. If you can't see its ribs like this, then your dog is much too fat.

Overweight dogs live a passive life, they play too little and tire quickly. They also suffer from all kinds of medical problems (problems in joints and heart conditions). They usually die younger too.

So it's important to make sure your dog doesn't get too fat. Always follow the guidelines on food packaging. Adapt them if your dog is less active or gets lots of snacks. Try to make sure your dog gets plenty of exercise by playing and running with it as much as you can. If your dog starts to show signs of putting on weight you can switch to a low-calorie food. If it's really too fat and reducing its food quantity doesn't help, then a special diet is the only solution. Your vet can also advise you.

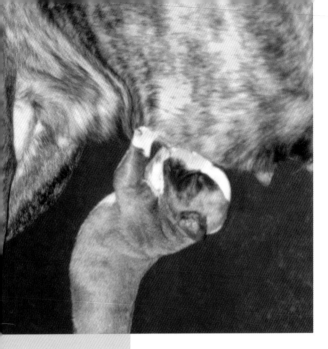

Caring for your Boxer

Good (daily) care is extremely important for your dog. A well cared-for dog is less likely to get sick. Caring for your dog is not only necessary but also a pleasure. Master and dog are giving each other some attention, and it's an excellent opportunity for a game and a cuddle.

The coat

Caring for your dog's coat involves regular brushing, together with checking for parasites such as fleas. Use the right equipment for taking care of the coat. Use a rubber or natural hairbrush. Always brush from head to tail along the direction of the coat.

If you get a puppy used to being brushed from an early age, it will enjoy having its coat cared for. Only bath a dog when it's really necessary. Always use a special dog shampoo and make sure it doesn't get into the dog's eyes or ears. Rinse the suds out thoroughly. Only let your dog outdoors again when it's completely dry. Even dogs can catch colds!

A vet can prescribe special medicinal shampoos for some skin conditions. Always follow the instructions to the letter.

Good flea prevention is highly important to avoid skin and coat problems. Fleas must be treated not only on the dog itself but also in its surroundings (see the chapter on Parasites). Coat problems can also occur due to an allergy to certain food substances. In such cases, a vet can prescribe a hypo-allergenic diet.

Teeth

A dog must be able to eat properly to stay in good condition, so it needs healthy teeth. Check its teeth regularly. Get in touch with your vet if you suspect that all is not well. Regular feeds of hard comes after you've been calling it a long time, then reward it. If you're angry because you had to wait so long, it may feel it's actually being punished for coming. It will probably not obey at all the next time for fear of punishment.

Try to take no notice of undesirable behaviour. Your dog will perceive your reaction (even a negative one) as a reward for this behaviour. If you need to correct the dog, then do this immediately. Use your voice or grip it by the scruff of its neck and push it to the ground. This is the way a mother dog calls her pups to order.

Rewards for good behaviour are, by far, preferable to punishment; they always get a better result.

House-training
The very first training (and one of the most important) that a dog needs is house-training. The basis for good house-training is keeping a good eye on your puppy. If you pay attention, you will notice that it will sniff a long time and turn around a certain spot before doing its business there. Pick it up gently and place it outside, always at the same place. Reward it abundantly if it does its business there.

Another good moment for house-training is after eating or sleeping. A puppy often needs to do its business at these times. Let it relieve itself before playing with it, otherwise it will forget to do so and you'll not reach your goal. For the first few days, take your puppy out for a walk just after it's eaten or woken up. It will quickly learn the meaning, especially if it's rewarded with a dog biscuit for a successful attempt. Of course, it's not always possible to go out after every snack or snooze. Lay newspapers at different spots in the house.

Whenever the pup needs to do its business, place it on a newspaper. After some time it will start to look for a place itself. Then start to reduce the number of newspapers until there is just one left, at the front or back door. The puppy will learn to go to the door if it defensive reaction. In this case try to resolve the dog's fear as far as possible. Reward it for letting you get to the painful spot. Be careful, because a dog in pain may also bite its master! Muzzling it can help prevent problems if you have to do something that may be painful. Never punish a dog for this type of aggression!

Fear

The source of anxious behaviour can often be traced to the first weeks of a dog's life. A shortage of new experiences during this important phase (also called the 'socialisation phase') has great influence on its later behaviour. A dog that never encountered humans, other dogs or animals during the socialisation phase will be afraid of them later. This fear is common in dogs brought up in a barn or kennel, with almost no contact with humans. As we saw, fear can lead to aggressive behaviour, so it's important that a puppy gets as many new impressions as possible in the first weeks of its life. Take it with you into town in the car or on the bus, walk it down busy streets and allow it to have plenty of contact with people, other dogs and other animals.

It's a huge task to turn an anxious, poorly socialised dog into a real pet. It will probably take an enormous amount of attention, love, patience and energy to get such an animal used to everything around it. Reward it often and give it plenty of time to adapt and, over time, it will learn to trust you and become less anxious. Try not to force anything, because that will always have the reverse effect. Here too, an obedience course can help a lot. A dog can be especially afraid of strangers. Have visitors give it something tasty as a treat. Put a can of dog biscuits by the door so that your visitors can spoil your dog when they arrive. Here again, don't try to force anything. If the dog is still frightened, leave it in peace.

Dogs are often frightened in certain situations; well-known examples are thunderstorms and fireworks. In these cases try to ignore their anxious behaviour. If you react to a dog's whimpering and whining, it's the same as rewarding it. If you ignore its fear completely, your dog will quickly learn that nothing is wrong. You can speed up this 'learning process' by rewarding its positive behaviour.

Rewarding

Rewarding forms the basis for bringing up a dog. Rewarding good behaviour works far better than punishing bad behaviour and rewarding is also much more fun. Recently, the opinions on raising dogs have gradually changed. In the past the proper way to correct bad behaviour was regarded as a sharp pull on the lead.

Today, experts view rewards as a positive incentive to get dogs to do what we expect of them. There are many ways to reward a dog. The usual ways are a stroke or a friendly word, even without a tasty treat to go with it. Of course, a piece of dog biscuit does wonders when you're training a puppy. Be sure you always have something delicious in your pocket to reward good behaviour.

Another form of reward is play. Whenever a dog notices that you have a ball in your pocket, it won't go far from your side. As soon as you've finished playing, put the ball away. This way your dog will always do its best in exchange for a game.

Despite the emphasis you put on rewarding good behaviour, a dog can sometimes be a nuisance or disobedient. You must correct such behaviour immediately. Always be consistent: once 'no' must always be 'no'.

Barking

Dogs which bark too much and too often are a nuisance for their surroundings. A dog-owner may tolerate barking up to a point, but neighbours are often annoyed by the unnecessary noise. Don't encourage your puppy to bark and yelp. Of course, it should be able to announce its presence, but if it goes on barking it must be called to order with a strict

'Quiet!'. If a puppy fails to obey, just hold its muzzle closed with your hand.

A dog will sometimes bark for long periods when left alone. It feels threatened and tries to get someone's attention by barking. There are special training programmes for this problem, where dogs learn that being alone is nothing to be afraid of, and that their master will always return.

You can practise this with your dog at home. Leave the room and come back in at once. Reward your dog if it stays quiet. Gradually increase the length of your absences and keep rewarding it as long as it remains quiet. Never punish the dog if it does bark or yelp. It will never understand punishment afterwards, and this will only make the problem worse. Never go back into the room as long as your dog is barking, as it will view this as a reward. You might want to make the dog feel more comfortable by switching the radio on for company during your absence. It will eventually learn that you always come back and the barking will reduce. If you don't get the required result, attend an obedience course.

Breeding

Dogs, and thus Boxers, follow their instincts, and reproduction is one of nature's important processes. For people who enjoy breeding dogs this is a positive circumstance.

Those who simply want a 'cosy companion' however, do not need the regular adventures with females on heat and unrestrainable males. Knowing a little about breeding in dogs will help you to understand why they behave the way they do, and the measures you need to take when this happens.

Liability

Breeding dogs is much more than simply 1+1= many. If you're planning to breed with your Boxer, be on your guard, otherwise the whole affair can turn into a financial drama because, under the law, a breeder is liable for the 'quality' of his puppies.

The breeder clubs place strict conditions on animals used for breeding. They must be examined

for possible congenital defects (see the chapter Your Boxer's health). This is the breeder's first obligation, and if you breed a litter and sell the puppies without these checks having been made, you may be held liable by the new owners for any costs arising from any inherited defects. These (veterinary) costs can be enormous!
So contact the breed association if you plan to breed a litter of Boxers.

The female in season

Bitches become sexually mature at about eight to twelve months. Then they go into season for the first time. They are 'on heat' for two to three weeks. During this period they discharge little drops of blood and they are very attractive to males. The bitch is fertile during the second half of

her season, and will accept a male to mate. The best time for mating is then between the ninth and thirteenth day of her season. A female's first season is often shorter and less severe than those that follow. If you do want to breed with your female you must allow this first (and sometimes the second) season to pass. Most bitches go into season twice per year.

If you do plan to breed with your Boxer in the future, then sterilisation is not an option to prevent unwanted offspring. A temporary solution is a contraceptive injection, although this is controversial because of side effects such as womb infections.

Phantom pregnancy

A phantom pregnancy is a not uncommon occurrence. The female behaves as if she has a litter. She takes all kinds of things to her basket and treats them like puppies. Her teats swell and sometimes milk is actually produced. The female will sometimes behave aggressively towards people or other animals, as if she is defending her young.

Phantom pregnancies usually begin two months after a season and can last a number of weeks. If it happens to a bitch once, it will often then occur after every season. If she suffers under it, sterilisation is the best solution, because continual phantom pregnancies increase the risk of

womb or teat conditions. In the short term a hormone treatment is worth trying, perhaps also homeopathic medicines. Camphor spirit can give relief when teats are heavily swollen, but rubbing the teats with ice or a cold cloth (moisten and freeze) can also help relieve the pain. Feed the female less than usual, and make sure she gets enough attention and extra exercise.

Preparing to breed

If you do plan to breed a litter of puppies, you must first wait for your female to be physically and mentally full-grown. In any event you must let her first season pass. To mate a bitch, you need a male. You could simply let her out on the street and she will quickly return home pregnant.

But if you have a pure-bred Boxer bitch, then it certainly makes sense to mate her with the best possible candidate, even if she has no pedigree. Proceed with caution and think especially about the following: Accompanying a bitch through pregnancy, birth and the first eight to twelve weeks afterwards is a time-consuming affair. Never breed with Boxers that have congenital defects, and this also applies to dogs without papers. The same goes for hyperactive, nervous and shy dogs. Mate your pedigree Boxer bitch with a dog that also has a pedigree. For more information, contact your local breed club secretary.

Pregnancy

It's often difficult to tell at first when a bitch is pregnant. Only after about four weeks can you feel the pups in her womb. She will now slowly get fatter and her behaviour will usually change. Her teats will swell during the last few weeks of pregnancy. The average pregnancy lasts 63 days, and costs her a lot of energy. In the beginning she is fed her normal amount of food, but her nutritional needs increase in jumps during the second half of the pregnancy. Give her approximately fifteen percent more food each week from the fifth week on. The mother-to-be needs extra energy and proteins during this phase of her pregnancy. During the last weeks you can give her a concentrated food, rich in energy, such as dry puppy food. Divide this into several small portions per day, because she can no longer deal with large portions of food. Towards the end of the pregnancy, her energy needs can easily be one-and-a-half times more than usual.

After about seven weeks the mother will start to demonstrate nesting behaviour and to look for a place to give birth to her young. This might be her own basket or a special whelping box. This must be ready at least a week before the birth to give the mother time to get used to it. The basket or box should preferably be in a quiet place.

The birth

The average litter is between three and nine puppies. The birth usually passes without problems. Of course, you must contact your vet immediately if you suspect a problem!

Suckling

After birth, the mother starts to produce milk. The suckling period is very demanding. During the first three to four weeks the pups rely entirely on their mother's milk. During this time she needs extra food and fluids. This can be up to three or four times the normal amount. If she's producing too little milk, you can give both mother and her young special puppy milk. Here too, divide the high quantity of food the mother needs over several smaller portions. Again, choose a concentrated, high-energy, food and give her plenty of fresh drinking water, but not cow's milk, which can cause diarrhoea.

You can give the puppies some supplemental solid food when they are three to four weeks old. There are special puppy foods available that follow on well from the mother's milk and can easily be eaten with their milk teeth.

Ideally, the puppies are fully weaned at an age of six or seven weeks, i.e. they no longer drink their mother's milk. The mother's milk production gradually stops and her food needs also drop.

Within a couple of weeks after weaning, the mother should again be getting the same amount of food as before the pregnancy.

Castration and sterilisation

As soon as you are sure your bitch should never bear a (new) litter, a sterilisation is the best solution. During sterilisation the uterus is removed in an operation. The bitch no longer goes into season and can never become pregnant. The best age for a sterilisation is about eighteen months, when the bitch is more or less fully grown.

A male dog is usually only castrated for medical reasons or to correct undesirable sexual behaviour. During a castration the testicles are removed, which is a simple procedure and usually without complications. There is no special age for castration but, where possible, wait until the dog is fully grown.

Vasectomy is sufficient where it's only a case of making the dog infertile. In this case the dog keeps its sexual drive but can no longer reproduce.

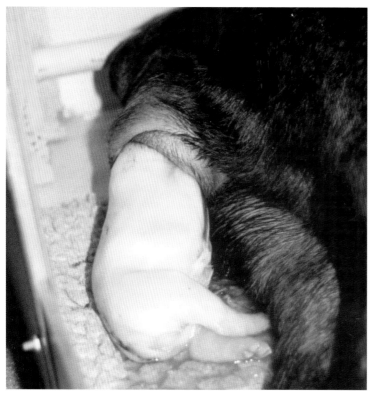

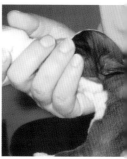

Sports and shows

A Boxer is an energetic dog and likes to be busy. It is often used for diverse sporting tasks, but officially it is a working dog breed, which means it is entitled to participate in the international guard dog examinations.

Many kennel clubs run their own agility competitions and championships. If you regularly participate in activities with your Boxer, you will not only realise that the bond between master and dog has grown stronger, but also that your dog is quieter and more obedient at home.

Agility

Agility is a form of dog sport that the Boxer can enjoy to its heart's content. In this discipline, the dog has to run through a course. The art is to do this as fast as possible with as few penalty points as possible. The obstacles consist of a slalom, a seesaw, a tunnel, hurdles and a fence. The dog, spurred on by its master, must take all the obstacles correctly. The dog with the fastest time and

the least penalty points is the winner. The sport is demanding on dog and master and they both need to be very fit.

Flyball

The Boxer will also enjoy this form of sport. In competitions, teams of four dogs face each other in the arena. The dogs must jump across four obstacles. They then reach a device with a narrow plank on the front. By pressing this plank with their paws they launch a (tennis) ball. They must then pick up the ball and bring it to their master as fast as possible. The team that has four balls first is the winner.

Behaviour and obedience

You can pick from a whole range of obedience training courses, beginning with a puppy course. Boxers usually enjoy this type of course. Their strong will to please means they want to perform the exercises as well as possible. After elementary obedience courses, you can train your dog for various behaviour and obedience diplomas.

Endurance test

This is primarily an European dog activity but dogs that have once learned to run alongside a bicycle usually enjoy it. And moreover, it's good for their muscle development and their body moves smoothly. Their muscles grow stronger without over-burdening their vulnerable joints. This is something that can be done along a canal towpath or along a country trail – not on a public road though. Never let your Boxer run beside the bike before it's a year old. Starting too young is bad for the development of its bones. Slowly build up the distance. Don't go out with a bike when it's too warm, don't feed your dog shortly beforehand and don't go too far. Advanced Boxers can take part in endurance competitions. The dog has to cover a distance of twenty kilometres beside the bicycle, at a speed between fifteen and twenty kilometres per hour.

A tunnel in an agility course

Road safety

Especially useful are road safety courses for dogs. Here, your Boxer can learn a few obedience exercises and at the end of the course can show you how safely it conducts itself in traffic.

Advanced working tests with the Boxer

In principle, a Boxer can perform various tasks, but by nature it is a real guard dog. In Europe 'schutz-hund' training and examination is a serious form of dog sports. It is held in four levels: A, I, II, and III. Each examination consists of three elements: tracking, obedience and arrest work. It is a difficult training that places high demands on dog and master. The arrest work is a spectacular part, but the dog must be very obedient before it can do these exercises. Many people think that dogs are made untrustworthy by arrest work, however the opposite is the case: the dog must be very disciplined throughout the exercise and high standards of obedience are required.

Tracker dog

A Boxer is also a very talented tracker dog and some top winning show dogs have been good tracking dogs. Although it may not look difficult at first sight, tracking is heavy and intensive work for a dog.
For the examination, the dog must show how sure it can track by following a scent that is two kilometres long and at least three hours old. There are seven bends in the track and it is crossed by two fresh "diversionary" scents well apart from each other. There are also seven objects on the track at varying intervals.

Exhibitions and exemption shows

Visiting a dog show is a pleasant experience for both dog and master, and for some dog-lovers it is an intensive hobby. They visit countless shows every year. Others find it nice to visit an exemption show with their dog just once. It's worth making the effort to visit an exemption show where a judge's experienced eyes will inspect your Boxer and assess it for form, gait, condition and behaviour. The judge's report will teach you your dog's weak and strong points, which may help you when choosing a mate for breeding. You can also exchange experiences with other Boxer owners. Official dog shows are only open to dogs with a pedigree.

Ring training and club events

If you've never been to a dog show, you will probably be fumbling in the dark in terms of what will be expected of you and your dog. Many Boxer and general dog clubs organise so-called ring training courses for dogs going to a show for the first time.

This training teaches you exactly what the judge will be looking for, and you can practise this together with your dog.

Open shows

All dog clubs organise dog shows. You must enter your dog in advance in a certain class. These meetings are usually small and friendly and are often the first acquaintance dog and master make with a "real" judge. This is an overwhelming experience for your dog - a lot of its contemporaries and a strange man or woman who fiddles around with it and peers into its mouth. After a few times, your dog will know exactly what's expected of it and will happily go to the next club match.

Championship shows

Various championship shows take place during the course of the year with different prizes. These shows are much more strictly organised than club matches. Your dog must be registered in a certain class in advance and it will then be listed in a catalogue. On the day itself, the dog is usually kept on a bench until its turn comes up. During the judging in the ring, it's important that you show your dog at its best. The judge examines each dog in turn. When all the dogs from that class have been judged, the best are selected and placed. After all the judging has finished, all the winners of the same sex in the various classes compete for the Challenge Certificate

(3 Challenge Certificates from different judges, and your Boxer will be a champion in the UK).The best Boxer in the eyes of the judge gets this award. Finally, the winners of each sex compete for the title of Best in Show. Of course, your dog must look very smart for the show. The judge will not be impressed if its coat is not clean, and its paws are dirty. Nails must be clipped and teeth free of plaque. The dog must also be free of parasites and ailments. A bitch must not be in season and a male must be in possession of both testicles. Apart from those things, judges also hate badly brought-up, anxious or nervous dogs. Get in touch with your local dog club or the breed association if you want to know more about shows.

Don't forget!
If you're planning to take your dog to a club match or in fact to any show, you need to be well prepared. Don't forget the following:

For yourself:
- Show documents if they have been sent to you
- Food and drink
- Clip for the catalogue number
- Chairs if an outside show

For your dog:
- Food and water bowls and food
- Dog blanket and perhaps a cushion
- Show lead
- A brush
- A benching chain and collar

Parasites

All dogs are vulnerable to various sorts of parasite. Parasites are tiny creatures that live at the expense of another animal. They feed on blood, skin and other body substances. There are two main types.

Internal parasites live within their host animal's body (tapeworm and roundworm) and external parasites live on the animal's exterior, usually in its coat (fleas and ticks), but also in its ears (ear mite).

Fleas

Fleas feed on a dog's blood. They cause not only itching and skin problems, but can also carry infections such as tapeworm. In large numbers they can cause anaemia and dogs can also become allergic to a flea's saliva, which can cause serious skin conditions. So it's important to treat your dog for fleas as effectively as possible, not just on the dog itself but also in its surroundings. For treatment on the animal, there are various medicines: drops for the neck and to put in its food, flea collars, long-life sprays and flea powders. There are various sprays in pet shops that can be used to eradicate fleas in the dog's immediate surroundings. Choose a spray that kills both adult fleas and their larvae.

If your dog goes in your car, you should spray that too. Fleas can also affect other pets, so you should treat those too. When spraying a room, cover any aquarium or fishbowl. If the spray reaches the water, it can be fatal for your fish!

Your vet and pet shop have a wide range of flea treatments and can advise you on the subject.

Flea

Ticks

Ticks are small, spider-like parasites. They feed on the blood of the animal or person they've settled on. A tick looks like a tiny, grey-coloured leather bag with eight feet. When it has sucked itself full, it can easily be five to ten times its own size and is darker in colour. Dogs usually fall victim to ticks in bushes, woods or long grass. Ticks cause not only irritation by their blood-sucking but can also carry a number of serious diseases. This applies especially to the Mediterranean countries, which can be infested with blood parasites. In our country these diseases are fortunately less common. But Lyme disease, which can also affect humans, has reached our shores. Your vet can prescribe a special treatment if you're planning to take your dog to southern Europe. It is important to fight ticks as effectively as possible. Check your dog regularly, especially when it's been running free in woods and bushes. It can also wear an anti-tick collar.

Removing a tick is simple using a tick pincette. Grip the tick with the pincette, as close to the dog's skin as possible, and carefully pull it out. You can also grip the tick between your fingers and, using a turning movement, pull it carefully out. You must disinfect the spot where the tick was using iodine to prevent infection. Never soak the tick in alcohol, ether or oil. In a shock reaction the tick may discharge the infected contents of its stomach into the dog's skin.

Tick

Worms

Dogs can suffer from various types of worm. The most common are tapeworm and roundworm. Tapeworm causes diarrhoea and poor condition. With a tapeworm infection you can sometimes find small pieces of the worm around the dog's anus or on its bed. In this case, the dog must be wormed. You should also check your dog for fleas, which carry the tapeworm infection.

Roundworm is a condition that reoccurs regularly. Puppies are often infected by their mother's milk. Your vet has medicines to prevent this. Roundworm causes problems (particularly in younger dogs), such as diarrhoea, loss of weight and stagnated growth. In serious cases the pup becomes thin, but with a swollen belly. It may vomit and you can then see the worms in its vomit. They are spaghetti-like tendrils. A puppy must be treated regularly for worms with a worm treatment. Adult dogs should be treated every six months.

Your Boxer's health

The room in this book is too limited to go into all the medical ups and downs of the Boxer. But we do want to give a little information on illnesses and deformities that affect this breed more often than other dogs.

Breed-specific conditions

Fortunately, most Boxers are healthy and happy dogs that can live to the age of ten or eleven. Although they do not get really old, they remain affectionate and playful until the end and are alert to events at home. We do confront some breed-specific conditions with the Boxer that are listed here.

Sensitive skin

Some Boxers have particularly sensitive skin, and appear to be particularly sensitive to injections. The dog will suddenly suffer a swelling on the head, which can conceal the eyes, and dense rashes over the whole body. A vet can prescribe anti-histamines to help the condition, sometimes the symptoms disappear on their own.

Tumours

Boxers are also vulnerable to all kinds of bumps and swellings, which may be malignant or not. Have your vet look at any swelling. Boxers can also get life-threatening cancer (tumours) such as skin tumours, gum tumours, brain tumours and leukaemia.

Back problems

Older Boxers, especially, can suffer from the vertebrae fusing. The whole back becomes as stiff as a plank, but as long as the dog is not in pain, it is not serious. Sometimes nerves seem to get trapped (hernia) and that does cause pain when the dog stands up and moves.

Respiration problems

Finally, most vets are reluctant to anaesthetise Boxers and other dogs with short snouts. During the anaesthetic, a cramp can easily occur in the vocal cords whereby the dog may be unable to breathe properly and can suffocate.

Stomach torsion

This is a turning over of the stomach and can occur after a heavy meal in combination with romping and exercise immediately after eating. This dangerous condition almost only affects large and medium-sized breeds. Symptoms of stomach torsion are:
• the dog tries to vomit, but fails;
• the dog is restless and walks with a raised back;
• pale mucous membranes;
• whining;
• a swelling is noticeable on the left side behind the ribs, which feels soft.

Only a small percentage of dogs with stomach torsion survive, and only after the fast intervention of a vet. This dangerous condition can be avoided by splitting the daily amount of food over at least two portions and allowing the dog to rest after each meal.

Hip Dysplasia (HD)

Boxers, as many other breeds, are vulnerable to HD. Although in this country we tend not to do much about Hip Dysplasia, we should be aware of what it is. Hip Dysplasia is a development disorder in the hip joint, which only becomes apparent after birth.

With this condition, the hip socket doesn't properly enclose the head of the thighbone. This causes inflammation and bone tumours, which can be very painful. Until recently, it was assumed that HD was primarily caused by genetic factors. Recent investigations, however, indicate that while genetic factors certainly play a role in terms of a dog's susceptibility to HD, external factors such as food quality and exercise appear at least equally important. Limit the chance of HD as far as possible by giving your dog ready-made food of a good brand, and don't add any supplements! Make sure your dog doesn't get too fat. A Boxer pup should be somewhat protected from HD in its first year. Don't let it romp too much with other dogs, chase sticks and balls too wildly or run up and down stairs. These kinds of games cause the pup to make abrupt and risky movements, which can overburden its soft joints.

Hip x-ray

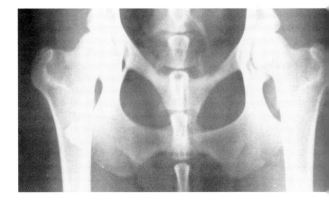

One important but under-estimated factor behind HD is the floor in your home. Parquet and tiled floors are much too slippery for a young dog. Regular slipping can cause complications that promote HD. If you have a smooth floor, it's advisable to lay blankets or old carpet in places the dog uses regularly. Let it spend lots of time in the garden as grass is a perfect surface to run on.

The Boxer project

In 1994, the Dutch Boxer Club and the veterinary faculty at the University of Utrecht started a large-scale genetic-epidemiological study. The research is intended to find out which diseases, including hereditary conditions, occur in Boxers and what environmental aspects play a role, including food, worming, vaccinations and living in a kennel or indoors.

The study began with a check of puppies that were born in 1994 and 1995. The owners of these dogs keep a special logbook and regularly answer questionnaires; permanent employees at the faculty are intensively involved in evaluating these. With all the data collected, they hope to get a lot of information about hereditary sickness patterns. They also expect to be able to give advice on avoidance of risks within breeding pair combinations given by breeders. Counselling then began

in mid-2000. This study is unique, both in the Netherlands and elsewhere. Of course, it's important that every Boxer-lover cooperates to get the best possible results. The breeders that are members of the Boxer Club of the Netherlands have dedicated themselves to that.

Heart problems

Some boxers do have heart problems in the form of two main conditions :

Aortic stenosis is a condition which obstructs blood flow through the major blood vessel - the aorta. Dogs' hearts are graded as to their effiency by a qualified veterinary surgeon. It is recommended that the parents of your puppy have been heart tested and they should have achieved a grade of 0 or 1.

Cardiomyopathy is another heart disease. This affects the functioning and ultimately the structure of the heart. Its ability to contract and relax becomes progressively impaired. Some dogs can live a long time and have an apparently healthy life but it is a progressive disease and a heart weakness. Once started it worsens with time and eventually will lead to heart failure. The research into this is only in the initial stages but it is advisable to talk to the breeder of the puppy about this condition, and to the breed club secretaries.

Trent Boxer Club
Sec. Mrs Wendy Brooks
Tel - 01507 472156
E-mail - Jinnybrux@aol.com
Contact Address - Jinnybrux
Bungalow, Lysheen, Alford Road,
Mablethorpe,
Lincolnshire, LN12 1PX.

Mancunian Boxer Club
Sec. Mrs Sandra Jump
Tel: 01606 889043
E-mail: boxer@quart.u-net.com
Contact Address - Watling House,
Forest Hill, Hartford, Northwich,
Cheshire, CW8 2AT.

Scottish Boxer Club
Sec. Mr Walker G Miller
Tel: 01776 870211
E-mail: walkonbox@aol.com
Leswalt, Stranraerleswalt
Stranraer

Midland Boxer Club
Sec. Mr Nigel J Rallings
Tel: 01827 872064
Rose Cottage, Dog Lane
Bodymore Heath,
Sutton Coldfield, West Midlands

Merseyside Boxer Club
Sec. Mrs Marion McArdle
Tel: 0151 531 6361
E-mail: boxerdog@mcards.-
fsnet.co.uk
Contact Address - 12 Beeston
Drive, Sefton, Liverpool, L30 7QQ.
www.merseysideboxer.com

Northern Boxer Club
Secretary - Mrs Anne Simpson
Telephone - 01274 560068
E-mail - Anne@cdbhelp.demon.co.uk
Contact Address - Hilthorn, 7
Crossley View, Gilstead, Bingley,
West Yorkshire, BD16 4QZ.
Web site - www.northernboxer-
club.co.uk

South Wales Boxer Club
Sec. Mrs Gill Davies
Tel: 01600 860082
E-mail - gill@kenbru.-
freeserve.co.uk
Contact Address -The Mews
House, Llanishen, Chepstow,
Monmouthshire.
Web site - www.southwalesboxer-
club.org.uk

Tyne Wear & Tees
Boxer Club
Sec. Mrs Ros Jones
Tel: 01670 351201
E-mail: rosalie.jones9@
btinternet.com
19 Dunkeld Close
South Beach, Blyth
Northhumberland NE24 3SP

The Boxer

Official name:	Boxer
FCI-classification:	Group 2, pinchers, schnauzers and Swiss mountain dogs
Original tasks:	Guard dog
Shoulder height:	Male: max. 63 cm Bitch: max. 59 cm
Weight:	Male: 30 - 32 kg Bitch: 24 - 25 kg
Life expectancy:	8 to 10 years